First Facts®

Christmas around the World

Christmas in
MEXICO

by Cheryl L. Enderlein

CAPSTONE PRESS
a capstone imprint

First Facts are published by Capstone Press,
1710 Roe Crest Drive, North Mankato, Minnesota 56003
www.capstonepub.com

Library of Congress Cataloging-in-Publication Data
Enderlein, Cheryl L.
Christmas in Mexico / by Cheryl L. Enderlein.
p. cm.—(First facts. Christmas around the world)
Includes bibliographical references and index.
Summary: "Describes the customs, songs, foods, and activities associated with the celebration of Christmas in Mexico"—Provided by publisher.
ISBN 978-1-62065-138-4 (library binding)
ISBN 978-1-4765-1061-3 (e-book PDF)
1. Christmas—Mexico—Juvenile literature. 2. Mexico—Social life and customs—Juvenile literature. I. Title.

GT4987.16.E54 2013
394.26630972—dc23   2012026287

Editorial Credits
Christine Peterson, editor; Ted Williams, designer; Eric Gohl, media researcher; Kathy McColley, production specialist

Photo Credits
AP Images: Eduardo Verdugo, cover; BigStockPhoto.com: holbox, 1; Capstone Studio: Karon Dubke, 21; Dreamstime: Hupeng, 11; Getty Images: LatinContent/Mario Castillo, 17; Newscom: Notimex/Francisco Santiago, 20, Notimex/Javier Lira, 6, Notimex/Jorge Gonzalez, 8, Notimex/Jose Luis Salmeron, 12, Photoshot/Xinhua/David de la Paz, 15, Zuma Press/El Universal, 5; Shutterstock: Nathalie Speliers Ufermann, 18

Design Elements: Shutterstock

Printed in the United States of America in North Mankato, Minnesota.
112015   009342R

TABLE OF CONTENTS

Christmas in Mexico

Music and children fill the streets. Bright red flowers decorate homes. Welcome to Christmas in Mexico! People around the world celebrate Christmas on December 25. But in Mexico, holiday celebrations begin on December 16 and end February 2. People celebrate Christmas with traditional music, food, and religious ceremonies.

How to Say It!

In Mexico people say *"Feliz Navidad"* (fay-LEEZ nah-vee-DAHD), which means "Happy Christmas."

Mexico

5

The First Christmas

Christmas is a **Christian** holiday celebrating the birth of **Jesus**. Long ago, Jesus' parents, Mary and Joseph, went to the Middle Eastern city of Bethlehem. The town was crowded, and they had no place to stay. They took shelter in a stable. There, Jesus was born. Poor shepherds and rich kings celebrated his birth.

Christian—a person who follows a religion based on the teachings of Jesus
Jesus—the founder of the Christian religion

Christmas Celebrations

Beginning on December 16, Mexicans celebrate Christmas with *posadas*. Children go door to door asking for a place to sleep.

posada—a Christmas festival that plays out Mary and Joseph's search for lodging

They carry small figures of Mary and Joseph. When people let them in, children give them the figures. Then everyone celebrates with a feast. Children crack open piñatas to get candy and gifts.

On Christmas Eve children lead a procession to church. They place a figure of baby Jesus in a church. On Christmas Day families go to church.

CHRISTMAS FACT!

After some Christmas Eve services, bells ring out and fireworks light up the sky.

Christmas Symbols

Holiday symbols such as poinsettias hold special meaning in Mexico. The plant is part of a Christmas story. A girl wanted to bring a gift to church for baby Jesus. But the girl was poor. So she picked some leaves from along the road as a gift. When she put the leaves by Jesus, they turned bright red.

CHRISTMAS FACT!

People call poinsettias "*Flores de Noche Buena*." This means "Flowers of the Holy Night."

Christmas Decorations

Bright lights and decorations fill homes and cities during Christmas in Mexico. People set out evergreens, poinsettias, and lilies. They make paper lanterns.

Families set up **nativities** in their homes. This scene includes figures of Mary, Joseph, and baby Jesus. It may also include figures of angels, shepherds, and animals.

nativity—a representation of the birth of Jesus

Santa Claus

Santa Claus is part of holiday celebrations in Mexico's larger cities. He brings gifts on Christmas Eve.

But for most children, it is the Three Kings who bring presents. These kings brought gifts to Jesus in Bethlehem. In Mexico the Kings bring gifts on January 6. This day marks the **Epiphany,** the country's main Christmas celebration.

Epiphany—a Christian festival celebrated on January 6 to mark the Three Kings' visit to baby Jesus

CHRISTMAS FACT!

Saint Nicholas was the first Santa Claus. He secretly gave gifts to children and poor people.

15

Christmas Presents

Imagine your shoes filled with candy and gifts. That's what children in Mexico wake up to on January 6. Before the holiday kids write letters asking the Three Kings for gifts. On January 5, kids put their shoes on a windowsill before going to bed. When they wake up, they find their shoes filled with presents from the Three Kings.

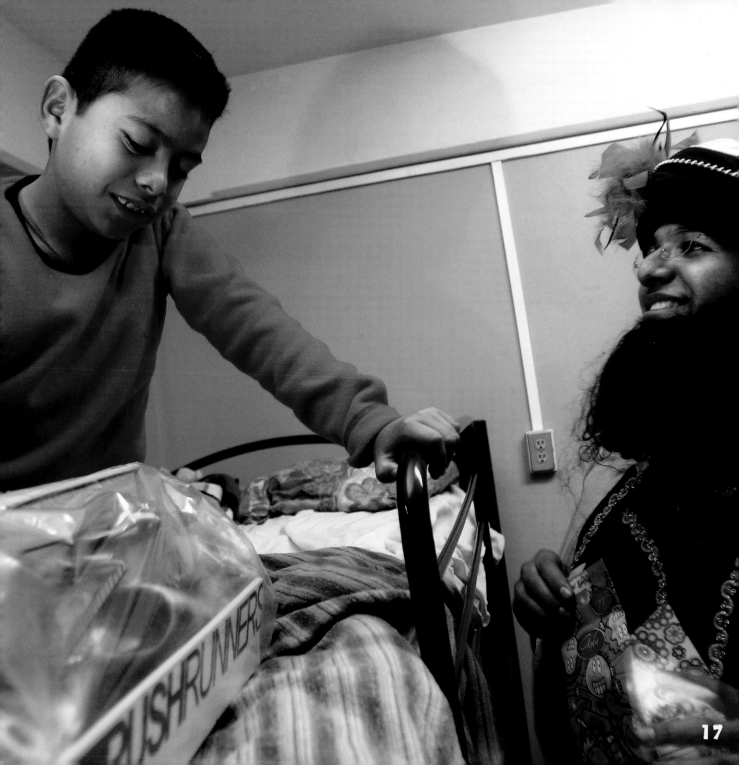

CHRISTMAS FACT!

A small figure of baby Jesus is hidden in the bread. Whoever finds the figure must host a party on February 2.

Christmas Food

Tortillas, sweetbread, and hot chocolate. Christmas is a delicious time in Mexico. On Christmas Day people enjoy turkey, tortillas, and a fruit and vegetable salad. Mexicans make a sweetbread called *Rosca de Reyes* on January 6. This ring-shaped treat is topped with candied fruit and served with hot chocolate.

Christmas Songs

In Mexico children sing special songs during posadas. At each house they sing a song asking for a place to stay. Through song, the owner either turns them away or welcomes them inside. Children also sing a lullaby to baby Jesus.

Hands-On:
MAKE A PIÑATA

Children across Mexico celebrate Christmas by making and breaking a piñata. You can make a piñata for your holiday party.

What You Need

- 1 round balloon
- measuring cup
- 1½ cups (360 mL) white school glue
- ½ cup (120 mL) water
- mixing bowl
- spoon
- newspapers
- red, green, and white paint
- string

What You Do

1. Blow up the balloon. Have an adult help you tie the end.
2. Measure the glue and water. Pour both into a mixing bowl and stir.
3. Tear newspapers into long strips about 2 inches (5 centimeters) wide. Dip a newspaper strip into the glue mixture until it is covered completely.
4. Stick the newspaper strip onto the balloon. Continue adding strips to the balloon until it is covered with three layers of newspaper. Let the balloon dry.
5. When dry, paint the piñata red, green, and white—the colors of Mexico.
6. When the paint dries, pop the balloon. Tie a string to the top of the piñata. Fill the piñata with candy, toys, and small gifts and have friends help break it open.

GLOSSARY

Christian (KRIS-chuhn)—a person who follows a religion based on the teachings of Jesus

Epiphany (ih-PIF-uh-nee)—a Christian festival celebrated on January 6 to mark the Three Kings' visit to baby Jesus

Jesus (JEE-zuhs)—the founder of the Christian religion; Christians believe that Jesus is the son of God

nativity (nuh-TIV-i-tee)—a representation of the birth of Jesus

posada (poh-SAH-duh)—a Christmas festival that plays out Mary and Joseph's search for lodging

READ MORE

Hardyman, Robyn. *Celebrate Mexico.* Celebrate. New York: Chelsea Clubhouse, 2009.

Peppas, Lynn. *Cultural Traditions in Mexico.* Cultural Traditions in My World. New York: Crabtree Pub. Co., 2012.

Trunkhill, Brenda. *Christmas around the World.* St. Louis: Concordia Publishing House, 2009.

INTERNET SITES

FactHound offers a safe, fun way to find Internet sites related to this book. All of the sites on FactHound have been researched by our staff.

Here's all you do:

Visit *www.facthound.com*

Type in this code: 9781620651384

Check out projects, games and lots more at
www.capstonekids.com

23

INDEX